For Elise

et al

An Anthology of Verse

selected by

E C Croydon

ISBN: 9783748172413

Printed and Published by Books on Demand GmbH
In de Tarpen 42, D-22848 Norderstedt
E-Mail: info@bod.de
Published by S Quast

Contents

Holy Sonnets:
Death, be not proud
John Donne (1572-1631)

Death, be not proud, though some have called
thee

Mighty and dreadful, for thou art not so;

For those whom thou think'st thou dost
overthrow

Die not, poor Death, nor yet canst thou kill me.

From rest and sleep, which but thy pictures be,

Much pleasure; then from thee much more
must flow,

And soonest our best men with thee do go,

Rest of their bones, and soul's delivery.

Thou art slave to fate, chance, kings, and
desperate men,

And dost with poison, war, and sickness dwell,

And poppy or charms can make us sleep as
well

And better than thy stroke; why swell'st thou
then?

One short sleep past, we wake eternally

And death shall be no more;

Death, thou shalt die.

Shadows in the Water
Thomas Traherne (1637-1674)

In unexperienced infancy

Many a sweet mistake doth lie:

Mistake though false, intending true;

A seeming somewhat more than view;

That doth instruct the mind

In things that lie behind,

And many secrets to us show

Which afterwards we come to know.

Thus did I by the water's brink

Another world beneath me think;

And while the lofty spacious skies

Reversèd there, abused mine eyes,

I fancied other feet

Came mine to touch or meet;

As by some puddle I did play

Another world within it lay.

Beneath the water people drowned,

Yet with another heaven crowned,

In spacious regions seemed to go

As freely moving to and fro:

In bright and open space

I saw their very face;

Eyes, hands, and feet they had like mine;

Another sun did with them shine.

'Twas strange that people there should walk,

And yet I could not hear them talk:

That through a little watery chink,

Which one dry ox or horse might drink,

We other worlds should see,

Yet not admitted be;

And other confines there behold

Of light and darkness, heat and cold.

I called them oft, but called in vain;

No speeches we could entertain:

Yet did I there expect to find

Some other world, to please my mind.

I plainly saw by these

A new antipodes,

Whom, though they were so plainly seen,

A film kept off that stood between.

By walking men's reversèd feet

I chanced another world to meet;

Though it did not to view exceed

A phantom, 'tis a world indeed;

Where skies beneath us shine,

 And earth by art divine

Another face presents below,

Where people's feet against ours go.

Within the regions of the air,

Compassed about with heavens fair,

Great tracts of land there may be found

Enriched with fields and fertile ground;

Where many numerous hosts

In those far distant coasts,

For other great and glorious ends

Inhabit, my yet unknown friends.

O ye that stand upon the brink,

Whom I so near me through the chink

With wonder see: what faces there,

Whose feet, whose bodies, do ye wear?

I my companions see

In you another me.

They seemèd others, but are we;

Our second selves these shadows be.

Look how far off those lower skies

Extend themselves! scarce with mine eyes

I can them reach. O ye my friends,

What secret borders on those ends?

Are lofty heavens hurled

'Bout your inferior world?

Are yet the representatives

Of other peoples' distant lives?

Of all the playmates which I knew

That here I do the image view

In other selves, what can it mean?

But that below the purling stream

Some unknown joys there be

Laid up in store for me;

To which I shall, when that thin skin

Is broken, be admitted in.

The Tyger
William Blake (1757-1827)

Tyger Tyger, burning bright,

In the forests of the night;

What immortal hand or eye,

Could frame thy fearful symmetry?

In what distant deeps or skies.

Burnt the fire of thine eyes?

On what wings dare he aspire?

What the hand, dare seize the fire?

And what shoulder, & what art,

Could twist the sinews of thy heart?

And when thy heart began to beat,

What dread hand? and what dread feet?

What the hammer? what the chain,

In what furnace was thy brain?

What the anvil? what dread grasp,

Dare its deadly terrors clasp!

When the stars threw down their spears

And water'd heaven with their tears:

Did he smile his work to see?

Did he who made the Lamb make thee?

Tyger Tygcr burning bright,

In the forests of the night:

What immortal hand or eye,

Dare frame thy fearful symmetry?

Daffodils

William Wordsworth (1770-1850)

I wandered lonely as a cloud

That floats on high o'er vales and hills,

When all at once I saw a crowd,

A host, of golden daffodils;

Beside the lake, beneath the trees,

Fluttering and dancing in the breeze.

Continuous as the stars that shine

And twinkle on the milky way,

They stretched in never-ending line

Along the margin of a bay:

Ten thousand saw I at a glance,

Tossing their heads in sprightly dance.

The waves beside them danced; but they

Out-did the sparkling waves in glee:

A poet could not but be gay,

In such a jocund company:

I gazed—and gazed—but little thought

What wealth the show to me had brought:

For oft, when on my couch I lie

In vacant or in pensive mood,

They flash upon that inward eye

Which is the bliss of solitude;

And then my heart with pleasure fills,

And dances with the daffodils.

The Destruction Of Sennacherib

George Gordon Byron, 1788 - 1824

The Assyrian came down like the wolf on the
fold,
And his cohorts were gleaming in purple and
gold;
And the sheen of their spears was like stars on
the sea,
When the blue wave rolls nightly on deep
Galilee.

Like the leaves of the forest when Summer is
green,
That host with their banners at sunset were
seen;

Like the leaves of the forest when Autumn hath
blown,

That host on the morrow lay withered and
strown.

For the Angel of Death spread his wings on the
blast,

And breathed in the face of the foe as he
passed;

And the eyes of the sleepers waxed deadly and
chill,

And their hearts but once heaved, and for ever
grew still!

And there lay the steed with his nostril all
wide,

But through it there rolled not the breath of his
pride;
And the foam of his gasping lay white on the
turf,
And cold as the spray of the rock-beating surf.

And there lay the rider distorted and pale,
With the dew on his brow, and the rust on his
mail;
And the tents were all silent, the banners alone,
The lances unlifted, the trumpet unblown.

And the widows of Ashur are loud in their wail,
And the idols are broke in the temple of Baal;
And the might of the Gentile, unsmote by the
sword,

Hath melted like snow in the glance of the Lord.

The Lady of Shallot

1842 Version (Revised from 1833)
Alfred Lord Tennyson (1809-1892)

Part I.

On either side the river lie

Long fields of barley and of rye,

That clothe the wold and meet the sky;

And thro' the field the road runs by

To many-tower'd Camelot;

And up and down the people go,

Gazing where the lilies blow

Round an island there below,

The island of Shalott.

Willows whiten, aspens quiver,

Little breezes dusk and shiver

Thro' the wave that runs for ever

By the island in the river

Flowing down to Camelot.

Four gray walls, and four gray towers,

Overlook a space of flowers,

And the silent isle imbowers

The Lady of Shalott.

By the margin, willow-veil'd

Slide the heavy barges trail'd

By slow horses; and unhail'd

The shallop flitteth silken-sail'd

Skimming down to Camelot:

But who hath seen her wave her hand?

Or at the casement seen her stand?

Or is she known in all the land,

The Lady of Shalott?

Only reapers, reaping early

In among the bearded barley,

Hear a song that echoes cheerly

From the river winding clearly,

Down to tower'd Camelot:

And by the moon the reaper weary,

Piling sheaves in uplands airy,

Listening, whispers "'Tis the fairy

Lady of Shalott."

Part II.

There she weaves by night and day

A magic web with colours gay.

She has heard a whisper say,

A curse is on her if she stay

To look down to Camelot.

She knows not what the curse may be,

And so she weaveth steadily,

And little other care hath she,

The Lady of Shalott.

And moving thro' a mirror clear

That hangs before her all the year,

Shadows of the world appear.

There she sees the highway near

Winding down to Camelot:

There the river eddy whirls,

And there the surly village-churls,

And the red cloaks of market girls,

Pass onward from Shalott.

Sometimes a troop of damsels glad,

An abbot on an ambling pad,

Sometimes a curly shepherd-lad,

Or long-hair'd page in crimson clad,
Goes by to tower'd Camelot;
And sometimes thro' the mirror blue
The knights come riding two and two:
She hath no loyal knight and true,
The Lady of Shalott.

But in her web she still delights
To weave the mirror's magic sights,
For often thro' the silent nights
A funeral, with plumes and lights
And music, went to Camelot:
Or when the moon was overhead,
Came two young lovers lately wed;
"I am half-sick of shadows," said
The Lady of Shalott.

Part III.

A bow-shot from her bower-eaves,

He rode between the barley-sheaves,

The sun came dazzling thro' the leaves,

And flamed upon the brazen greaves

Of bold Sir Lancelot.

A redcross knight for ever kneel'd

To a lady in his shield,

That sparkled on the yellow field,

Beside remote Shalott.

The gemmy bridle glitter'd free,

Like to some branch of stars we see

Hung in the golden Galaxy.

The bridle-bells rang merrily

As he rode down to Camelot:

And from his blazon'd baldric slung

A mighty silver bugle hung,

And as he rode his armour rung,

Beside remote Shalott.

All in the blue unclouded weather

Thick-jewell'd shone the saddle-leather,

The helmet and the helmet-feather

Burn'd like one burning flame together,

As he rode down to Camelot.

As often thro' the purple night,

Below the starry clusters bright,

Some bearded meteor, trailing light,

Moves over still Shalott.

His broad clear brow in sunlight glow'd;

On burnish'd hooves his war-horse trode;

From underneath his helmet flow'd

His coal-black curls as on he rode,

As he rode down to Camelot.

From the bank and from the river

He flash'd into the crystal mirror,

"Tirra lirra," by the river

Sang Sir Lancelot.

She left the web, she left the loom,

She made three paces thro' the room,

She saw the water-lily bloom,

She saw the helmet and the plume,

She look'd down to Camelot.

Out flew the web and floated wide;

The mirror crack'd from side to side;

"The curse is come upon me," cried

The Lady of Shalott.

Part IV.

In the stormy east-wind straining,

The pale-yellow woods were waning,

The broad stream in his banks complaining,

Heavily the low sky raining

Over tower'd Camelot;

Down she came and found a boat

Beneath a willow left afloat,

And round about the prow she wrote

The Lady of Shalott.

And down the river's dim expanse –

Like some bold seër in a trance,

Seeing all his own mischance –

With a glassy countenance

Did she look to Camelot.

And at the closing of the day

She loosed the chain, and down she lay;

The broad stream bore her far away,

The Lady of Shalott.

Lying, robed in snowy white

That loosely flew to left and right –

The leaves upon her falling light –

Thro' the noises of the night

She floated down to Camelot:

And as the boat-head wound along

The willowy hills and fields among,

They heard her singing her last song,

The Lady of Shalott.

Heard a carol, mournful, holy,

Chanted loudly, chanted lowly,

Till her blood was frozen slowly,

And her eyes were darken'd wholly,

Turn'd to tower'd Camelot;

For ere she reach'd upon the tide

The first house by the water-side,

Singing in her song she died,

The Lady of Shalott.

Under tower and balcony,

By garden-wall and gallery,

A gleaming shape she floated by,

A corse between the houses high,

Silent into Camelot.

Out upon the wharfs they came,

Knight and burgher, lord and dame,

And round the prow they read her name,

The Lady of Shalott.

Who is this? and what is here?

And in the lighted palace near

Died the sound of royal cheer;

And they cross'd themselves for fear,

All the knights at Camelot:

But Lancelot mused a little space;

He said, "She has a lovely face;

God in his mercy lend her grace,

The Lady of Shalott."

The Passing of Arthur
Alfred Lord Tennyson (!809-1892)

And slowly answered Arthur from the barge:

The old order changeth, yielding place to new,

And God fulfils Himself in many ways,

Lest one good custom should corrupt the

world.

Comfort thyself: what comfort is in me?

I have lived my life, and that which I have done

May He within Himself make pure! but thou,

If thou shouldst never see my face again,

Pray for my soul. More things are wrought by

prayer

Than this world dreams of. Wherefore, let thy

voice

Rise like a fountain for me night and day.

For what are men better than sheep or goats
That nourish a blind life within the brain,
If, knowing God, they lift not hands of prayer
Both for themselves and those who call them
friend?
For so the whole round earth is every way
Bound by gold chains about the feet of God.
But now farewell. I am going a long way
With these thou seëst—if indeed I go
(For all my mind is clouded with a doubt)—
To the island-valley of Avilion;
Where falls not hail, or rain, or any snow,
Nor ever wind blows loudly; but it lies
Deep-meadowed, happy, fair with orchard-
lawns
And bowery hollows crowned with summer
sea,

Where I will heal me of my grievous wound.'
So said he, and the barge with oar and sail
Moved from the brink, like some full-breasted
swan
That, fluting a wild carol ere her death,
Ruffles her pure cold plume, and takes the
flood
With swarthy webs. Long stood Sir Bedivere
Revolving many memories, till the hull
Looked one black dot against the verge of
dawn,
And on the mere the wailing died away.

My Last Duchess
Robert Browning (1812 - 1889)

That's my last Duchess painted on the wall,

Looking as if she were alive. I call

That piece a wonder, now: Frà Pandolf's hands

Worked busily a day, and there she stands.

Will 't please you sit and look at her? I said

'Frà Pandolf' by design, for never read

Strangers like you that pictured countenance,

The depth and passion of its earnest glance,

But to myself they turned (since none puts by

The curtain I have drawn for you, but I)

And seemed as they would ask me, if they

durst,

How such a glance came there; so, not the first

Are you to turn and ask thus. Sir, 't was not

Her husband's presence only, called that spot

Of joy into the Duchess' cheek: perhaps

Frà Pandolf chanced to say, 'Her mantle laps

Over my lady's wrist too much,' or 'Paint

Must never hope to reproduce the faint

Half-flush that dies along her throat:' such stuff

Was courtesy, she thought, and cause enough

For calling up that spot of joy. She had

A heart—how shall I say?—too soon made

glad,

Too easily impressed; she liked whate'er

She looked on, and her looks went everywhere.

Sir, 't was all one! My favour at her breast,

The dropping of the daylight in the West,

The bough of cherries some officious fool

Broke in the orchard for her, the white mule

She rode with round the terrace—all and each

Would draw from her alike the approving speech,

Or blush, at least. She thanked men,—good! but thanked

Somehow—I know not how—as if she ranked

My gift of a nine-hundred-years-old name

With anybody's gift. Who'd stoop to blame

This sort of trifling? Even had you skill

In speech—(which I have not)—to make your will

Quite clear to such an one, and say, 'Just this

Or that in you disgusts me; here you miss,

Or there exceed the mark'—and if she let

Herself be lessoned so, nor plainly set

Her wits to yours, forsooth, and made excuse,

—E'en then would be some stooping; and I choose

Never to stoop. Oh, sir, she smiled, no doubt,
Whene'er I passed her; but who passed without
Much the same smile? This grew; I gave
commands;

Then all smiles stopped together.

There she stands
As if alive. Will't please you rise? We'll meet
The company below then. I repeat,
The Count your master's known munificence
Is ample warrant that no just pretence
Of mine for dowry will be disallowed;
Though his fair daughter's self, as I avowed
At starting, is my object. Nay, we'll go
Together down, sir. Notice Neptune, though,
Taming a sea-horse, thought a rarity,

Which Claus of Innsbruck cast in bronze for me!

Home Thoughts, from the Sea
By Robert Browning (1812-1889)

Nobly, nobly Cape Saint Vincent to the North-
West died away;
Sunset ran, one glorious blood-red, reeking into
Cadiz Bay;
Bluish 'mid the burning water, full in face
Trafalgar lay;
In the dimmest North-East distance, dawned
Gibraltar grand and gray;
"Here and here did England help me: how can I
help England?"—say,
Whoso turns as I, this evening, turn to God to
praise and pray,
While Jove's planet rises yonder, silent over
Africa.

Home Thoughts from Abroad

By Robert Browning (1812-1889)

Oh, to be in England

Now that April's there,

And whoever wakes in England

Sees, some morning, unaware,

That the lowest boughs and the brushwood

sheaf

Round the elm-tree bole are in tiny leaf,

While the chaffinch sings on the orchard bough

In England now!

And after April, when May follows,

And the whitethroat builds, and all the

swallows!

Hark, where my blossomed pear-tree in the
hedge
Leans to the field and scatters on the clover
Blossoms and dewdrops at the bent spray's
edge.
That's the wise thrush; he sings each song twice
over,
Lest you should think he never could recapture
The first fine careless rapture!
And though the fields look rough with hoary
dew,
All will be gay when noontide wakes anew
The buttercups, the little children's dower
Far brighter than this gaudy melon-flower!

Song
(When I am dead, my dearest)
Christina Rosetti (1830 - 1894)

When I am dead, my dearest,

Sing no sad songs for me;

Plant thou no roses at my head,

Nor shady cypress tree:

Be the green grass above me

With showers and dewdrops wet;

And if thou wilt, remember,

And if thou wilt, forget.

I shall not see the shadows,

I shall not feel the rain;

I shall not hear the nightingale

Sing on, as if in pain:

And dreaming through the twilight

That doth not rise nor set,

Haply I may remember,

And haply may forget.

My Shadow
Robert Louis Stevenson (1850-1894)

I have a little shadow that goes in and out with
me,

And what can be the use of him is more than I
can see.

He is very, very like me from the heels up to
the head;

And I see him jump before me, when I jump
into my bed.

The funniest thing about him is the way he
likes to grow—

Not at all like proper children, which is always
very slow;

For he sometimes shoots up taller like an India-rubber ball,

And he sometimes gets so little that there's
none of him at all.

He hasn't got a notion of how children ought to
play,
And can only make a fool of me in every sort
of way.
He stays so close beside me, he's a coward you
can see;
I'd think shame to stick to nursie as that
shadow sticks to me!

One morning, very early, before the sun was
up,
I rose and found the shining dew on every
buttercup;

But my lazy little shadow, like an arrant sleepy-head,

Had stayed at home behind me and was fast asleep in bed.

The Windhover

Gerard Manly Hopkins (1844-1889)

To Christ Our Lord

I caught this morning morning's minion,

kingdom of daylight's dauphin, dapple-dawn-

drawn Falcon, in his riding

Of the rolling level underneath him steady air,

and striding

High there, how he rung upon the rein of a

wimpling wing

In his ecstasy! then off, off forth on swing,

As a skate's heel sweeps smooth on a bow-

bend: the hurl and gliding

Rebuffed the big wind. My heart in hiding

Stirred for a bird, – the achieve of, the mastery

of the thing.

Brute beauty and valour and act, oh, air, pride,

plume, here

Buckle! AND the fire that breaks from thee

then, a billion

Times told lovelier, more dangerous, O my

chevalier!

No wonder of it: shéer plód makes plough

down sillion

Shine, and blue-bleak embers, ah my dear,

Fall, gall themselves, and gash gold-vermilion.

Clancy of the Overflow

Andrew Barton "Banjo" Paterson (1864-1941)

I had written him a letter which I had, for want
of better

knowledge, sent to where I met him down the

Lachlan years ago;

He was shearing when I knew him, so I sent the

letter to him,

Just on spec, addressed as follows, "Clancy, of

The Overflow."

And an answer came directed in a writing

unexpected

(And I think the same was written with a

thumb-nail dipped in tar);

'Twas his shearing mate who wrote it, and

verbatim I will quote it:

"Clancy's gone to Queensland droving,

and we don't know where he are."

In my wild erratic fancy visions come to me of

Clancy

Gone a-droving "down the Cooper" where the

Western drovers go;

As the stock are slowly stringing, Clancy rides

behind them singing,

For the drover's life has pleasures that the

townsfolk never know.

And the bush has friends to meet him, and their

kindly voices greet him

In the murmur of the breezes and the river on

its bars,

And he sees the vision splendid of the sunlit
plain extended,
And at night the wondrous glory of the
everlasting stars.

I am sitting in my dingy little office, where a
stingy   ray of sunlight struggles feebly down
between the houses tall,
And the foetid air and gritty of the dusty, dirty
city,
through the open window floating, spreads its
foulness over all.

And in place of lowing cattle, I can hear the
fiendish rattle
of the tramways and the buses making hurry
down the street;
And the language uninviting of the gutter

children fighting

comes fitfully and faintly through the ceaseless

tramp of feet.

And the hurrying people daunt me, and their

pallid faces haunt me

as they shoulder one another in their rush and

nervous haste,

With their eager eyes and greedy, and their

stunted forms and weedy,

for townsfolk have no time to grow, they have

no time to waste.

And I somehow rather fancy that I'd like to

change with Clancy,

like to take a turn at droving where the seasons

come and go,

While he faced the round eternal of the cash-
book and the journal -
But I doubt he'd suit the office, Clancy, of The
Overflow.

The Ballad of the Drover
Henry Lawson (1867-1922)

ACROSS the stony ridges,

Across the rolling plain,

Young Harry Dale, the drover,

Comes riding home again.

And well his stock-horse bears him,

And light of heart is he,

And stoutly his old pack-horse

Is trotting by his knee.

Up Queensland way with cattle

He travelled regions vast;

And many months have vanished

Since home-folk saw him last.

He hums a song of someone

He hopes to marry soon;

And hobble-chains and camp-ware

Keep jingling to the tune.

Beyond the hazy dado

Against the lower skies

And yon blue line of ranges

The homestead station lies.

And thitherward the drover

Jogs through the lazy noon,

While hobble-chains and camp-ware

Are jingling to a tune.

An hour has filled the heavens

With storm-clouds inky black;

At times the lightning trickles

Around the drover's track;

But Harry pushes onward,

His horses' strength he tries,

In hope to reach the river

Before the flood shall rise.

The thunder from above him
Goes rolling o'er the plain;
And down on thirsty pastures
In torrents falls the rain.
And every creek and gully
Sends forth its little flood,
Till the river runs a banker,
All stained with yellow mud.

Now Harry speaks to Rover,
The best dog on the plains,
And to his hardy horses,
And strokes their shaggy manes;
'We've breasted bigger rivers
When floods were at their height
Nor shall this gutter stop us
From getting home to-night!'

The thunder growls a warning,

The ghastly lightnings gleam,

As the drover turns his horses

To swim the fatal stream.

But, oh! the flood runs stronger

Than e'er it ran before;

The saddle-horse is failing,

And only half-way o'er!

When flashes next the lightning,

The flood's grey breast is blank,

And a cattle dog and pack-horse

Are struggling up the bank.

But in the lonely homestead

The girl will wait in vain —

He'll never pass the stations

In charge of stock again.

The faithful dog a moment

Sits panting on the bank,

And then swims through the current

To where his master sank.

And round and round in circles

He fights with failing strength,

Till, borne down by the waters,

The old dog sinks at length.

Across the flooded lowlands

And slopes of sodden loam

The pack-horse struggles onward,

To take dumb tidings home.

And mud-stained, wet, and weary,

Through ranges dark goes he;

While hobble-chains and tinware

Are sounding eerily.

*****

The floods are in the ocean,

The stream is clear again,

And now a verdant carpet

Is stretched across the plain.

But someone's eyes are saddened,

And someone's heart still bleeds

In sorrow for the drover

Who sleeps among the reeds.

Lepanto

G K Chesterton (1874-1936)

White founts falling in the courts of the sun,

And the Soldan of Byzantium is smiling as

they run;

There is laughter like the fountains in that face

of all men feared,

It stirs the forest darkness, the darkness of his

beard,

It curls the blood-red crescent, the crescent of

his lips,

For the inmost sea of all the earth is shaken

with his ships.

They have dared the white republics up the

capes of Italy,

They have dashed the Adriatic round the Lion

of the Sea,

And the Pope has cast his arms abroad for
agony and loss,

And called the kings of Christendom for
swords about the Cross,

The cold queen of England is looking in the
glass;

The shadow of the Valois is yawning at the
Mass;

From evening isles fantastical rings faint the
Spanish gun,

And the Lord upon the Golden Horn is
laughing in the sun.

Dim drums throbbing, in the hills half heard,

Where only on a nameless throne a crownless
prince has stirred,

Where, risen from a doubtful seat and half

attainted stall,

The last knight of Europe takes weapons from
the wall,

The last and lingering troubadour to whom the
bird has sung,

That once went singing southward when all the
world was young,

In that enormous silence, tiny and unafraid,

Comes up along the winding road the noise of
the Crusade.

Strong gongs groaning as the guns boom far,

Don John of Austria is going to the war,

Stiff flags straining in the night-blasts cold

In the gloom black-purple, in the glint old-gold.

Torchlight crimson on the copper kettle-drums,

Then the tuckets, then the trumpets, then the
cannon, and he comes.

Don John laughing in the brave beard curled,

Spurning of his stirrups like the throne of all
the world,

Holding his head up for a flag of all the free.

Love-light of Spain -- hurrah!

Death-light of Africa!

Don John of Austria

Is riding to the sea.

Mahound is in his paradise above the evening
star,

(*Don John of Austria is going to the war.*)

He moves a mighty turban on the timeless
houri's knees,

His turban that is woven of the sunset and the
seas.

He shakes the peacock gardens as he rises from
his ease,

And he strides among the tree-tops and is taller
than the trees,
And his voice through all the garden is a
thunder sent to bring
Black Azrael and Ariel and Ammon on the
wing.
Giants and the Genii,
Multiplex of wing and eye,
Whose strong obedience broke the sky
When Solomon was king.

They rush in red and purple from the red clouds
of the morn,
From temples where the yellow gods shut up
their eyes in scorn;
They rise in green robes roaring from the green
hells of the sea

Where fallen skies and evil hues and eyeless
creatures be;
On them the sea-valves cluster and the grey
sea-forests curl,
Splashed with a splendid sickness, the sickness
of the pearl;
They swell in sapphire smoke out of the blue
cracks of the ground,--
They gather and they wonder and give worship
to Mahound.
And he saith, `Break up the mountains where
the hermit-folk can hide,
And sift the red and silver sands lest bone of
saint abide,
And chase the Giaours flying night and day, not
giving rest,

For that which was our trouble comes again out of the west.

We have set the seal of Solomon on all things under sun,

Of knowledge and of sorrow and endurance of things done,

But noise is in the mountains, in the mountains, and I know

The voice that shook our palaces -- four hundred years ago:

It is he that saith not `Kismet'; it is he that knows not Fate;

It is Richard, it is Raymond, it is Godfrey at the gate!

It is he whose loss is laughter when he counts the wager worth,

Put down your feet upon him, that our peace be
on the earth.'
For he heard drums groaning and he heard guns
jar,
(*Don John of Austria is going to the war.*)
Sudden and still -- hurrah!
Bolt from Iberia!
Don John of Austria
Is gone by Alcalar.

St Michael's on his mountain in the sea-roads
of the north
(*Don John of Austria is girt and going forth.*)
Where the grey seas glitter and the sharp tides
shift
And the sea folk labour and the red sails lift.
He shakes his lance of iron and he claps his
wings of stone;

The noise is gone through Normandy; the noise
is gone alone;

The North is full of tangled things and texts
and aching eyes

And dead is all the innocence of anger and
surprise,

And Christian killeth Christian in a narrow
dusty room

And Christian dreadeth Christ that hath a newer
face of doom,

And Christian hateth Mary that God kissed in
Galilee,

But Don John of Austria is riding to the sea.

Don John calling through the blast and the
eclipse

Crying with the trumpet, with the trumpet of
his lips,
Trumpet that sayeth ha!
Domino gloria!
Don John of Austria
Is shouting to the ships.

King Philip's in his closet with the Fleece about
his neck
(*Don Juan of Austria is armed upon the deck.*)
The walls are hung with velvet that is black and
soft as sin,
And little dwarfs creep out of it and little
dwarfs creep in.
He holds a crystal phial that has colours like
the moon,
He touches, and it tingles, and he trembles very
soon,

And his face is as a fungus of a leprous white and grey
Like plants in the high houses that are shuttered from the day,
And death is in the phial; and the end of noble work,
But Don John of Austria has fired upon the Turk.
Don John's hunting, and his hounds have bayed --
Booms away past Italy the rumour of his raid
Gun upon gun, ha! ha!
Gun upon gun, hurrah!

Don John of Austria
Has loosed the cannonade.

The Pope was in his chapel before day or battle broke,

(Don John of Austria is hidden in the smoke.)

The hidden room in man's house where God sits all the year,

The secret window whence the world looks small and very dear.

He sees as in a mirror on the monstrous twilight sea

The crescent of his cruel ships whose name is mystery;

They fling great shadows foe-wards, making Cross and Castle dark,

They veil the plumèd lions on the galley's of St. Mark;

And above the ships are palaces of brown, black-bearded chiefs,

And below the ships are prisons, where with multitudinous griefs,

Christian captives sick and sunless, all a labouring race repines

Like a race in sunken cities, like a nation in the mines.

They are lost like slaves that swat, and in the skies of morning hung

The stair-ways of the tallest gods when tyranny was young.

They are countless, voiceless, hopeless as those fallen or fleeing on

Before the high Kings' horses in the granite of Babylon.

And many a one grows witless in his quiet room in hell

Where a yellow face looks inward through the

lattice of his cell,

And he finds his God forgotten, and he seeks
no more a sign --

(*But Don John of Austria has burst the battle-
line!*)

Don John pounding from the slaughter-painted
poop,

Purpling all the ocean like a bloody pirate's
sloop,

Scarlet running over on the silvers and the
golds,

Breaking of the hatches up and bursting of the
holds,

Thronging of the thousands up that labour
under sea

White for bliss and blind for sun and stunned

for liberty.

Vivat Hispania!

Domino Gloria!

Don John of Austria

Has set his people free!

Cervantes on his galley sets the sword back in
the sheath

(*Don John of Austria rides homeward with a
wreath.*)

And he sees across a weary land a straggling
road in Spain,

Upon which a lean and foolish knight forever
rides in vain,

And he smiles, but not as Sultans smile, and
settles back the blade...

(*But Don John of Austria rides home from the
Crusade.*)

Snake

David Herbert Lawrence (1885-1930)

A snake came to my water-trough

On a hot, hot day, and I in pyjamas for the heat,

To drink there.

In the deep, strange-scented shade of the great

dark carob tree

I came down the steps with my pitcher

And must wait, must stand and wait, for there

he was at the trough before me.

He reached down from a fissure in the earth-

wall in the gloom

And trailed his yellow-brown slackness soft-

bellied down, over the edge of the stone trough

And rested his throat upon the stone bottom,
And where the water had dripped from the tap,
in a small clearness,
He sipped with his straight mouth,
Softly drank through his straight gums, into his
slack long body,
Silently.

Someone was before me at my water-trough,
And I, like a second-comer, waiting.

He lifted his head from his drinking, as cattle
do,
And looked at me vaguely, as drinking cattle
do,
And flickered his two-forked tongue from his
lips, and mused a moment,
And stooped and drank a little more,
Being earth-brown, earth-golden from the

burning bowels of the earth

On the day of Sicilian July, with Etna smoking.

The voice of my education said to me

He must be killed,

For in Sicily the black, black snakes are

innocent, the gold are venomous.

And voices in me said, If you were a man

You would take a stick and break him now, and

finish him off.

But must I confess how I liked him,

How glad I was he had come like a guest in

quiet, to drink at my water-trough

And depart peaceful, pacified, and thankless,

Into the burning bowels of this earth?

Was it cowardice, that I dared not kill him?
Was it perversity, that I longed to talk to him?

Was it humility, to feel honoured?
I felt so honoured.

And yet those voices:
If you were not afraid you would kill him.

And truly I was afraid, I was most afraid,
But even so, honoured still more
That he should seek my hospitality
From out the dark door of the secret earth.

He drank enough
And lifted his head, dreamily, as one who has
drunken,

And flickered his tongue like a forked night on the air, so black,

Seeming to lick his lips,

And looked around like a god, unseeing, into the air,

And slowly turned his head,

And slowly, very slowly, as if thrice adream,

Proceeded to draw his slow length curving round

And climb again the broken bank of my wall-face.

And as he put his head into that dreadful hole,

And as he slowly drew up, snake-easing his shoulders, and entered further,

A sort of horror, a sort of protest against his withdrawing into that horrid black hole,

Deliberately going into the blackness, and

slowly drawing himself after,

Overcame me now his back was turned.

I looked round, I put down my pitcher,

I picked up a clumsy log

And threw it at the water-trough with a clatter.

I think it did not hit him,

But suddenly that part of him that was left

behind convulsed in undignified haste,

Writhed like lightning, and was gone

Into the black hole, the earth-lipped fissure in

the wall-front,

At which, in the intense still noon, I stared with

fascination.

And immediately I regretted it.

I thought how paltry, how vulgar, what a mean
act!

I despised myself and the voices of my
accursèd human education.

And I thought of the albatross,

And I wished he would come back, my snake.

For he seemed to me again like a king,

Like a king in exile, uncrowned in the
underworld,

Now due to be crowned again.

And so, I missed my chance with one of the
lords
Of life.

And I have something to expiate:

A pettiness.

The Soldier
Rupert Brook (1887-1915)

If I should die, think only this of me:

   That there's some corner of a foreign field

That is for ever England. There shall be

   In that rich earth a richer dust concealed;

A dust whom England bore, shaped, made

aware,

   Gave, once, her flowers to love, her ways to

roam,

A body of England's, breathing English air,

   Washed by the rivers, blest by suns of home.

And think, this heart, all evil shed away,

   A pulse in the eternal mind, no less

   Gives somewhere back the thoughts by

England given;

Her sights and sounds; dreams happy as her day;

And laughter, learnt of friends; and gentleness,

In hearts at peace, under an English heaven.

(BLACK MARIGOLDS)
THE CHAURAPANCHASIKA by CHAURAS
translated by Edward Powys Mathers
(1892-1939)

Even now
My thought is all of this gold-tinted king's
daughter

With garlands tissue and golden buds,

Smoke tangles of her hair, and sleeping or
waking

Feet trembling in love. full of pale langour;

My thought is clinging as to a lost learning

Slipped down out of the minds of men,

Labouring to bring her back into my soul.

Even now

If I see in my soul the citron-breasted fair one

Still gold-tinted, her face like our night stars,

Drawing unto her; her body beaten about with flame,

Wounded by the flaring spear of love,

My first of all by reason of her fresh years,

Then is my heart buried alive in snow.

Even now

If my girl with lotus eyes came to me again

Weary with the dear weight of young love,

Again I would give her to these starved twins of arms

And from her mouth drink down the heavy wine,

As a reeling pirate bee in fluttered ease

Steals up the honey from the nenuphar.

Even now

I bring her back, ah, wearied out with love

So that her slim feet could not bear her up;

Curved falls of her hair down on her white cheeks;

In the confusion of her coloured vests

Speaking that guarded giving up, and her scented arms

Lay like cool bindweed over against my neck.

Even now

I bring her back to me in her quick shame,

Hiding her bright face at the point of day:

Making her grave eyes move in watered stars,
For love's great sleeplessness wandering all night,

Seeming to sail gently, as that pink bird,

Down the water of love in a harvest of lotus.

Even now

If I saw her lying all wide eyes

And with collyrium the indent of her cheek

Lengthened to the bright ear and her pale side

So suffering the fever of my distance,

Then would my love for her be ropes of
flowers, and night

A black-haired lover on the breasts of day.

Even now

I see the heavy startled hair of this reed-flute
player

Who curved her poppy lips to love dances,
Having a youth's face madding like the moon

Lying at her full; limbs ever moving a little in
love,

Too slight, too delicate, tired with the small
burden

Of bearing love ever on white feet.

Even now

She is present to me on her beds,

Balmed with the exhaltation of a flattering
musk,

Rich with the curdy essence of santal;

Girl with eyes dazing as the seeded wine,

Showing as a pair of gentle nut-hatches

Kissing each other with their bills, each hidden

By turns within a little grasping mouth.

Even now

She swims back in the crowning hour of love

All red with wine her lips have given to drink,

Soft round the mouth with camphor and faint
blue

Tinted upon the lips, her slight body,

Her great live eyes, the colourings of herself

A clear perfection; sighs of musk outstealing

And powdered wood spice heavy of Cashmir.

Even now

I see her; far face blond like gold

Rich with small lights, and tinted shadows
surprised

Over and over all of her; with glittering eyes

All bright for love but very love weary,

As it were the conjuring disk of the moon when
Rahou ceases

With his dark stumbling block to hide her rays.

Even now

She is art-magically present to my soul,
And that one word of strange heart's ease,
goodbye,

That in the night, in loth moving to go,

And bending over to a golden mouth,

I said softly to the turned away
Tenderly tired hair of this king's daughter.

Even now

My eyes that hurry to see no more are painting,
painting

Faces of my lost girl. O golden rings

That tap against cheeks of small magnolia
leaves,

O whitest so soft parchment where

My poor divorced lips have written excellent

Stanzas of kisses, and will write no more.

Even now

Death sends me the flickering of powdery lids

Over wild eyes and the pity of her slim body

All broken up with the weariness of joy;

The little red flowers of her breasts to be my comfort

Moving above scarves, and for my sorrow

Wet crimson lips that once I marked as mine.

Even now

By a cool noise of waters in the spring

The Asoka with young flowers that feign her fingers

And bud in red; and in the green vest pearls kissing

As it were rose leaves in the gardens of God; the shining at night

Of white cheeks in the dark; smiles from light thoughts within,

And her walking as of a swan: these trouble me.

Even now

The pleased intimacy of rough love

Upon the patient glory of her form

Racks me with memory; and her bright dress

As it were a yellow flame, which the white hand

Shamefastly gathers in her rising haste,

The slender grace of her departing feet.

Even now

When all my heavy heart is broken up

I seem to see my prison walls breaking

And then a light, and in that light a girl

Her fingers busied about her hair, her cool white arms

Faint rosy at the elbows, raised in the sunlight,

And temperate eyes that wander far away.

Even now

I seem to see my prison walls come close,

Built up of darkness, and against that darkness

A girl no taller than my breast and very tired,

Leaning upon the bed and smiling, feeding

A little bird and lying slender as ash trees,

Sleepily aware as I told of the green

Grapes and the small bright coloured river flowers.

Even now

I see her, as I used, in her white palace

Under black torches throwing cool red light,

Woven with many flowers and tearing the dark.

I see her rising, showing all her face

Defiant timidly, saying clearly:

Now I shall go to sleep, good night, my ladies.

Even now

Though I am so far separate, a flight of birds

Swinging from side to side over the valley
trees,

Passing my prison with their calling and
crying,

Bring me to see my girl. For very bird-like

Is her song singing, and the state of a swan

In her light walking, like the shaken wings

Of a black eagle falls her nightly hair.

Even now

I know my princess was happy. I see her stand

Touching her breasts with all her flower-soft
fingers,

Looking askance at me with smiling eyes.

There is a god that arms him with a flower

And she was stricken deep. Here, oh die here.

Kiss me and I shall be purer than quick rivers.

Even now

They chatter her weakness through the two
bazaars

Who was so strong to love me. And small men

That buy and sell for silver being slaves

Crinkle the fat about their eyes; and yet

No Prince of the Cities of the Sea has taken
her,

Leading to his grim bed. Little lonely one,

You clung to me as a garment clings; my girl.

Even now

Only one dawn shall rise for me. The stars
Revolve to-morrow's night and I not heed.

One brief cold watch beside an empty heart

And that is all. This night she rests not well;

Oh, sleep; for there is heaviness for all the
world

Except for the death-lighted heart of me.

Even now

My sole concern the slipping of her vests,

Her little breasts the life beyond this life.

One night of disarray in her green hems,

Her golden cloths, outweighs the order of earth,

Making of none effect the tides of the sea.

I have seen her enter the temple meekly and
there seem

The flag of flowers that veils the very god.

Even now

I mind the coming and talking of wise men
from towers

Where they had thought away their youth. And
I, listening,

Found not the salt of the whispers of my girl,

Murmur of confused colours, as we lay near
sleep;

Little wise words and little witty words,

Wanton as water, honied with eagerness.

Even now

I call to mind her weariness in the morning

Close lying in my arms, and tiredly smiling

At my disjointed prayer for her small sake.

Now in my morning the weariness of death

Sends me to sleep. Had I made coffins

I might have lived singing to three score.

Even now

The woodcutter and the fishermen turn home,

With on his axe the moon and in his dripping
net

Caught yellow moonlight. The purple flame of
fires

Calls them to love and sleep. From the hot
town

The maker of scant songs for bread wanders

To lie under the clematis with his girl.

The moon shines on her breasts and I must die.

Even now

I have a need to make up prayers, to speak

My last consideration of the world

To the great thirteen gods, to make my balance

Ere the soul journeys on. I kneel and say:

Father of Light. Leave we it burning still

That I may look at you. Mother of the Stars,

Give me your feet to kiss; I love you, dear.

Even now

I seem to see the face of my lost girl

With frightened eyes, like a wood wanderer,

In travail with sorrowful waters, unwept tears

Labouring to be born and fall; when white face turned

And little ears caught at the far murmur,

The pleased snarling of the tumult of dogs

When I was hurried away down the white road.

Even now

When slow rose-yellow moons looked out at
night

To guard the sheaves of harvest and mark down
The peach's fall, how calm she was and love
worthy.

Glass-coloured starlight falling as thin as dew
Was wont to find us at the spirit's starving time

Slow straying in the orchard paths with love.

Even now

Love is a god and Rati the dark his bride;

But once I found their child and she was fairer,

That could so shine. And we were each to each

Wonderful and a presence not yet felt

In any dream. I knew the sunset earth

But as a red gold ring to bear my emerald

Within the little summer of my youth.

Even now

I marvel at the bravery of love.

She, whose two feet might be held in one hand

And all her body on a shield of the guards,

Lashed like a gold panther taken in a pit

Tearfully valiant, when I too was taken;

Bearding her black beard father in his wrath,

Striking the soldiers with white impotent
hands.

Even now

I mind that I loved cypress and roses, dear,

The great blue mountains and the small grey
hills,

The sounding of the sea. Upon a day

I saw strange eyes and hands like butterflies;

For me at morning larks flew from the thyme

And children came to bathe in little streams.

Even now

Sleep left me all these nights for your white
bed

And I am sure you sistered lay with sleep

After much weeping. Piteous little love,

Death is in the garden, time runs down,

The year that simple and unexalted ran till now

Ferments in winy autumn, and I must die.

Even now

I mind our going, full of bewilderment

As who should walk from sleep into great light,

Along the running of the winter river,

A dying sun on the cool hurrying tide

No more by green rushes delayed in dalliance,

With a clear purpose in his flower flecked
length

Informed, to reach Nirvana and the sea.

Even now

I love long black eyes that caress like silk,

Ever and ever sad and laughing eyes,

Whose lids make such sweet shadow when
they close

It seems another beautiful look of hers.

I love a fresh mouth, ah, a scented mouth,

And curving hair, subtle as a smoke,

And light fingers, and laughter of green gems.

Even now
I mind asking: Where love and how love Rati's
priestesses?

You can tell me of their washings at moon
down

And if that warm basin have silver borders.

Is it so that when they comb their hair

Their fingers, being purple stained, show

Like coral branches in the black sea of their
hair?

Even now

I remember that you made answer very softly,

We being one soul, your hand on my hair,

The burning memory rounding your near lips:

I have seen the priestesses of Rati make love at
moon fall

And then in a carpeted hall with a bright gold lamp

Lie down carelessly anywhere to sleep.

Even now

I have no surety that she is not Mahadevi

Rose red of Siva, or Kapagata

The wilful ripe Companion of the King,
Or Krisna's own Lakshmi, the violet haired.

I am not certain but that dark Brahma

In his high secret purposes

Has sent my soft girl down to make the three worlds mad

With capering about her scented feet.

Even now

Call not the master painters from all the world,

Their thin black boards, their rose and green
and grey,

Their ashes of lapis lazuli ultramarine,

Their earth of shadows the umber. Laughing at
art

Sunlight upon the body of my bride,

For painting not nor any eyes for ever.

Oh warm tears on the body of my bride.

Even now

I mind when the red crowds were passed and it
was raining

How glad those two that shared the rain with
me;

For they talked happily with rich young voices
And at the storm's increase, closer and with
content,

Each to the body of the other held

As there were no more severance for ever.

Even now

The stainless fair appearance of the moon

Rolls her gold beauty over an autumn sky

And the stiff anchorite forgets to pray;

How much the sooner I, if her wild mouth

Tasting of the taste of manna came to mind

And kept my soul at balance above a kiss.

Even now

Her mouth carelessly scented as with lotus dust

Is water of love to the great heat of love,
A tirtha very holy, a lover's lake

Utterly sacred. Might I go down to it

But one time more, then should I find a way

To hold my lake for ever and ever more

Sobbing out my life beside the waters.

Even now

I mind that the time of the falling of blossoms
starrted my dream

Into a wild life, into my girl;

Then was the essence of her beauty spilled

Down on my days so that it fades not,

Fails not, subtle and fresh, in perfuming

That day, and the days, and this the latest day.

Even now

She with young limbs as smooth as flower
pollen,

Whose swaying body is laved in the cool

Waters of langour, this dear bright-coloured
bird,

Walks not, changes not, advances not

Her weary station by the black lake

Of Gone Forever, in whose fountain vase

Balance the water-lilies of my thought.

Even now

Spread we our nets beyond the farthest rims

So surely that they take the feet of dawn

Before you wake and after you are sleeping

Catch up the visible and visible stars

And web the ports the strongest dreamer
dreamed,

Yet all is one, Vidya, yet it is nothing.

Even now

The night is full of silver straws of rain,

And I will send my sould to see your body

This last poor time. I stand beside your bed;

Your shadowed head lies leaving a bright space

Upon the pillow empty, your sorrowful arm

Holds from your side and clasps not anything.

There is no covering upon you.

Even now

I think your feet seek mine to comfort them.

There is some dream about you even now
Which I'll not hear at waking. Weep not at
dawn,

Though day brings wearily your daily loss

And all the light is hateful. Now is it time

To bring my soul away.

Even now

I mind that I went round with men and women,

And underneath their brows, deep in their eyes,

I saw their souls, which go slipping aside

In swarms before the pleasure of my mind;

The world was like a flight of birds, shadow or flame

Which I saw pass above the engraven hills.

Yet was there never one like to my girl.

Even now

Death I take up as consolation.

Nay, were I free as the condor with his wings

Or old kings throned on violet ivory,

Night would not come without beds of green floss

And never a bed without my bright darling.

It is most fit that you strike now, black guards,

And let this fountain out before the dawn.

Even now

I know that I have savoured the hot taste of life

Lifting green cups and gold at the great feast.

Just for a small and a forgotten time

I have had full in my eyes from off my girl

The whitest pouring of eternal light.

The heavy knife. As to a gala day.

Notes: